Lost and Found

by **Jennifer Smith Turner**

with art by **Valarie Smith**

Also by Jennifer Smith Turner

Perennial Secrets, Poetry & Prose

Lost and Found

Rhyming Verse
Honoring African American Heroes

by Jennifer Smith Turner
with art by Valarie Smith

ISBN-13: 978-0-9790817-0-5
ISBN-10: 0-9790817-0-X

Library of Congress Control Number: 2006909936

This book is printed on acid free paper.

First Edition

Printed in the United States of America

Art ©2006 by Valarie Smith
Cover Design by Jennifer Smith Turner
Author's Photograph Copyrighted by John Groo

Published by Connecticut River Press in collaboration with Morning Dove Press
To order copies contact:

Connecticut River Press
111 Holmes Road
Newington, CT 06111
860-666-0615
www.morningdovepress.com

Dedicated to Eric

Acknowledgements

Valarie Smith, my sister, is the artist who created the wonderful images throughout the book. We have done much together: as youngsters playing in the Boston neighborhood of Jamaica Plain, our childhood home; to vacationing summers on Martha's Vineyard as adults; to standing by our mother's side as she took her last breath. Our collaboration in creating this book – my verse, her drawings – makes me see two young girls walking hand-in-hand, kicking up colorful leaves on a blissful walk home from school.

A special acknowledgement to the people depicted in these drawings and verse, those still with us and those who have joined the ancestors – you make our world better.

Introduction

Each of the individuals on these pages has special meaning for me. I have a personal relationship with many, while others have touched my life by the courageous ways in which they lived their lives. However, the most significant hero is my mother, Margaree Smith, whose image is on the next page. Through her love of words, dedication to family, and magnificent vision, she taught me that the world has limitless possibilities. I believe she continues to watch over me, so I know she is proud of this book – a collaboration between her two daughters – which celebrates her along with those whom she admired during her lifetime.

Jennifer Smith Turner

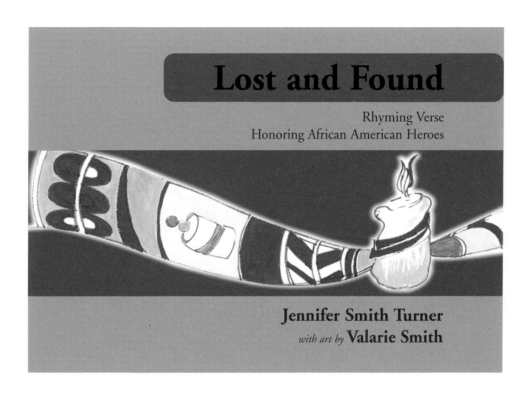

Lost and Found

Rhyming Verse
Honoring African American Heroes

Jennifer Smith Turner
with art by **Valarie Smith**

Found us today
Somewhere amid decay of yesterday
Yearning for new tomorrows.

Somewhere in the echo
Of moving stairs taking
Ghost shoppers nowhere
To stores, shops, food stands
No longer there.

Somewhere in posters
Dated April, May any year
However not today
Telling stories of triumph,
Solidarity, leadership
As well as people at play.

Stories defining who we are
Martin, Malcolm shake hands
Rosa, Aretha, Lauren Hill
Smile back – sigh
At the adjacent window's proclamation –

**THIS STORE NOW CLOSED
RETURNS….
GO SOMEWHERE ELSE.**

As thump,

Thump,

Thump,

Moving stairs

Raise no one

To enter there.

Our entire history reduced
To a bumper sticker, saying –
I have a dream…

Martin would not be pleased
To see his words, deeds
Breeze along highways
Stuck to dimpled metal chrome, by just anyone
No thought, understanding of any byways
Just two bucks to spare –
So unfair.

Found us today
Sitting in ivory towers
Windowless cubicles
Faceless walls –
Earning our pay.

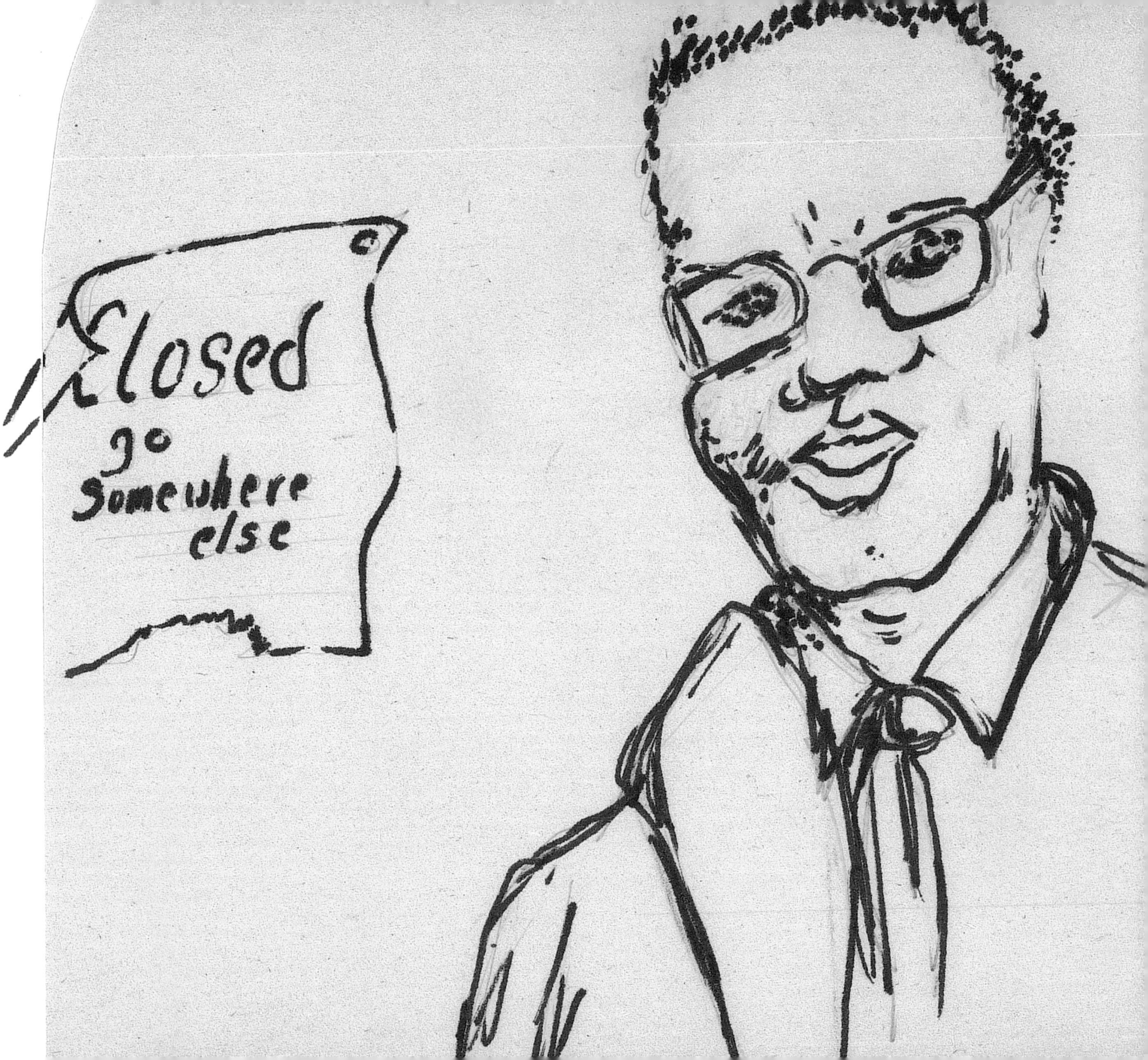
Closed
go
Somewhere
else

Malcolm would place an X beside these
Implore us – please…
Do not forget why we stood tall
Understand how we lived our lives
Be present today – for tomorrow's sake – please
Even while earning your pay…

Martin, Malcolm – we hear
And are quietly staking a place
Bolstered by ghosts
Always part of our day
Imprinting the future
With scenes from past plays
Each character signals the cue
To others on their way.

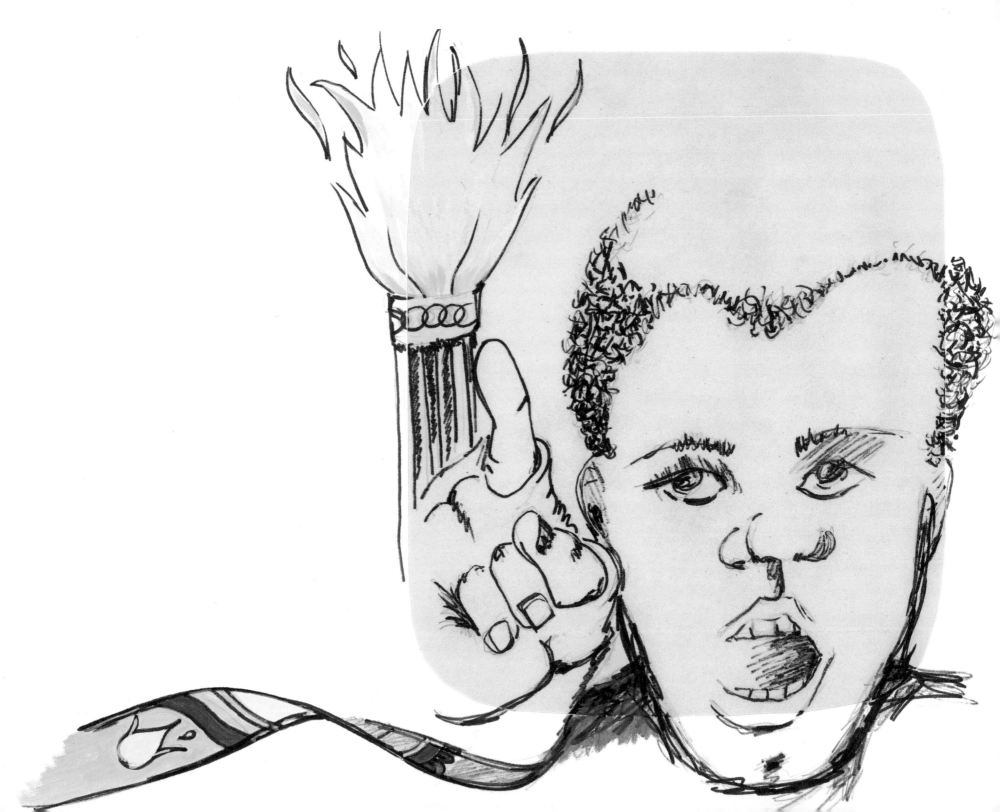

Float like a butterfly, sting like a bee
Muhammad Ali wants us to be
Light as air, solid as night, never afraid
Clear about that which is right…
Yesterday's cost – title fight
Today's legacy – champion to all
Such power in being forthright.

One hundred days
After gross Mississippi injustice
Emmett Till uneasy in his grave
Siren call rings loud –
Too tired to move out the way.

Rosa Parks tells us – *stay!*
Claim our place do not be put at bay
Room a-plenty for all who choose to come this way
In buses, in marches, on store-front counter stools
In schools, churches, government tables too
Not dogs, bullets, coarse rope noose or jim-crow laws
Kept us from heeding her momentous call.

Grace, commitment rules the day!
Dr. Dorothy Height has her say
We are inspired, we are in awe
Grace, charm can take one quite far
To tables never before acknowledging who you are
To nations informed only by media clips
To leaders moved to unsilence their lips
In the presence of your intellect, wit
You teach us much,
Have traveled so very far.

Dr. Maulana Karenga creates icons of culture
Teaches us to honor, pray, display
Stand tall in our own way
Seven principles he elucidates for us
Light each one on its extraordinary day –

Umoja – *I am because we are*
Kujichagulia – *self-determination as community*
Ujima – *collective responsibility*
Ujamaa – *cooperative economics*
Nia – *purpose for collective good*
Kuumba – *creativity*
Imani – *faith and triumph*

Nineteen sixty-six – a few thousand candles did light
Twenty-first century – millions,
Millions more shine bright.

Maya personifies phenomenal us
Proclaims joy, delight
In lives we share so much,
She might whisper:

Come sit by me child, right at my side
a story I will share,
at first will seem sad, yet listen real close
light of triumph you will soon discern there
in the hair on my head
sway of my hips
wink in my eye
as I leave a teasing kiss.

Her light shines so bright
Let it shine, let it shine, oh let it shine.

With refined, elegant touch
Arthur Ashe held court for us
Quiet words
Powerful thought
Strength in purpose –
He fought
Doors once closed – opened
Champion – redefined
Open path for William sisters
His life did design.

Three years beyond my birth
An icon passed away
She left these words along the way –

I leave you love
I leave you hope
I leave you the challenge
Of developing confidence
In one another
I leave you respect for
The use of power
I leave you faith
I leave you racial dignity…

Would have been proud
To know Mary McLeod Bethune
Must rely on knowledge of our history
To sing her and all others praise aloud
And in the singing come to know
Deep, rich, roots our heritage does sow.

Found us today
GenXers hip hopping along the way
Viewing elders in a peripheral way
Longing for guidance
While wanting to play
Creating the landscape
For Generation Y, right behind
Mirroring leaders from decades past
With skills honed in a world moving much too fast
Teaching those in our prime –
Never too aged to learn
From those we must not leave behind.

Found us today!

About the Heroes

Margaree L. Smith – (1928-2000) my mother.

Dr. Martin Luther King, Jr. – (1929-1968) was an inspirational leader of the Civil Rights Movement. His philosophical belief in racial justice through non-violence was a cornerstone of positive change in race relations in America during the nineteen sixties and beyond.

Malcolm X – (1925-1965) was a Black Muslim who stressed the importance of racial respect as a means to achieving societal respect. He embraced the concepts of Black Nationalism and self-help.

Muhammad Ali – (1942-) entered the national scene as one of the all-time boxing heavyweight champions in the world. When he refused to be inducted into the United States Army for religious reasons, he was stripped of his championship title and banned from boxing competitions. He is honored today for his strong convictions and outstanding athletic talent.

Emmett Till – (1941-1955) was a fourteen-year-old boy from Chicago visiting family in Mississippi in 1955. He was accused of whistling at a white woman while in a store and was subsequently beaten to death by a group of white men believed to be the Ku Klux Klan. His death was a catalyst for galvanizing people against racial hatred and bringing the horror of segregation to the forefront of America's consciousness.

Rosa Parks – (1913-2005) refused to move to the back of the bus and give her seat to a white man as required by segregation laws. Her act of defiance was the spark for the Montgomery, Alabama bus boycott and the birth of the Civil Rights Movement across the country.

Dr. Dorothy Height – (1912-) served as President of the National Council of Negro Women for several decades. She was involved with the National YWCA for many years and has been a tireless supporter of equal rights for women and African Americans. In 2004 she was awarded the Congressional Gold Medal by President George W. Bush.

Dr. Maulana Karenga – (1941-) is chairman of the Department of Black Studies at California State University, Long Beach. In 1966 he introduced Kwanzaa as an annual celebration of African American community, family, values, and culture. Kwanzaa is now a national tradition.

Dr. Maya Angelou – (1928-) is a world-renowned poet and author, who touches people's souls with her inspiring words.

Arthur Ashe – (1943-1993) is known for the important strides he made in breaking racial barriers in the professional tennis world. He also quietly worked to improve opportunities for African Americans in professional venues throughout corporate America.

Dr. Mary McLeod Bethune – (1875-1955) was an educator who founded the National Council of Negro Women and Bethune-Cookman College. The excerpt from her speech was found in a publication of the Schomburg Center for Research in Black Culture.

Generations X and Y – Our future…

Who are your heroes?

About the Artist

Valarie Smith

Valarie Smith is a talented visual artist who creates works in many mediums from acrylics, to ink-line drawings, to sculpture. She is also a world-renowned jewelry designer and served for many years as the in-house jewelry designer for an international jewelry firm. She was twice awarded the Japan Cultured Pearl Association's award for outstanding design. *The Modern Jeweler* recognized her designs with awards on six different occasions. Her artwork has been on display at many local and national galleries. Ms. Smith is a graduate of the University of Massachusetts, Dartmouth and has taken numerous courses at the Rhode Island School of Design. She resides in Massachusetts.

About the Author

Jennifer Smith Turner

Jennifer Smith Turner is a New England born writer. She began writing poetry thirty years ago while an English major at Union College in Schenectady, New York. She is the author of *Perennial Secrets, Poetry & Prose* published in 2003 and nominated for the 2004 Connecticut Book Awards. She was nominated for the Connecticut Poet Laureate appointment in 2006. Her range of verse is eclectic in the hundreds of poems she has written. Her work is included in *Vineyard Poets*, an anthology of poems by Martha's Vineyard writers and in numerous literary publications. She is a graduate of Union College, where she earned a Bachelors degree. She received her Masters degree from Fairfield University, Fairfield, Connecticut. Subsequent to her studies she spent twenty-eight years in corporate America holding numerous senior executive positions. She is a member of the Poetry Society of America, The Academy of American Poets, and serves on many boards of academic and non-profit organizations across the country. She presently serves as the President of the Board for the Hartford Stage Company. Jennifer resides in Connecticut and Martha's Vineyard with her husband.

www.jennifersmithturner.com

To arrange an Author Event:

Visit – www.jennifersmithturner.com and provide information under the "contact" tab or
Email – morningdovepress@earthlink.net

Order Form
(Cut and mail or fax)

Lost and Found, Rhyming Verse Honoring African American Heroes
by Jennifer Smith Turner

Number of Books _____ @ $22.00 = _____   (volume discounts available)
(Add $4 shipping/handling for
  one book, $2 for each additional   = _____
  book)
(CT. Residents add 6% sales tax $1.32 = _____
  per book)
                              Total $_____

Your Mailing Information:
Name: _____
Address:
_____
_____
Email/Phone: _____

Make check or money order payable to: **Smith & Associates, LLC**
Mail Or Fax To:
Connecticut River Press, 111 Holmes Road, Newington, CT 06111 Fax – 860-594-0736
Thank You!